Why the Ocean Is Salty

Written by Alice Leonhardt
Illustrated by Marilee Heyer

STECK-VAUGHN
ELEMENTARY · SECONDARY · ADULT · LIBRARY

A Harcourt Classroom Education Company

www.steck-vaughn.com

Contents

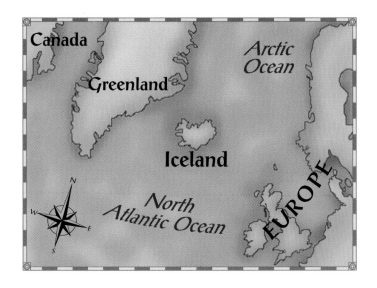

Introduction

hy is the ocean salty? Scientists tell us that the minerals in rocks are broken down by wind and weather. These minerals are washed into the sea. Some of them make the ocean salty.

Long ago there were no scientists. But even then people wondered why things are the way they are. To explain the world around them, people created pourquoi (poor KWAH) tales. *Pourquoi* is the French word for *why*. The pourquoi tale you are about to read comes from Iceland.

The Magic Millstones

A worried King Ari of Iceland stood on the shore of his island country. The waves crashed upon the rocky beach. The sky loomed as gray and cold as the dark, freezing water. In the distance ice bobbed on the waves of the North Atlantic Ocean. Seagulls flew overhead, crying mournfully as they searched for fish among the waves. "Where is spring?" they seemed to call. "Where are the gentle winds and warm ocean currents?"

Spring was late, and King Ari was troubled. Turning, he gazed at the land behind him. Instead of sheep grazing on new green grass, he saw only snow covering the hills. The branches of the trees were brown and bare. The frozen ground was too hard to be plowed.

"Papa!" cried Nina, the king's little daughter, as she came running along the beach toward him. He caught her in his arms and saw that her cheeks were hollow. Her blue eyes were huge in her thin face. "Where are the fish?" Nina asked. "Why don't they come to our shores again so we can catch them?"

"The water is too cold for the fish," King Ari explained. "They will arrive with the warm ocean currents."

"But it is spring, Papa," Nina insisted. "The fish should be here! Then I would not be hungry!"

King Ari hugged his daughter and sighed. His people had eaten almost all of the cabbage, turnips, and salted meats they had stored for the long winter. Soon they would have nothing to eat.

King Ari knew that something had to be done. He set up a meeting in the village. When he arrived, all the men were there. Dressed in their shaggy furs and leather boots, they huddled around a roaring fire.

"If spring doesn't come, my sheep will starve," one man said.

"If spring doesn't come, my cattle will starve," said another.

"If the ocean tides don't bring fish, my family and I will starve," said another.

King Ari raised his hand, commanding silence. "I know the winter has been long. I have tried to find a way to feed our families and our livestock," he said tiredly. "I cannot. I am afraid we must leave our island home."

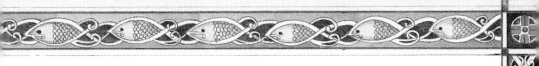

King Ari's words scared and angered the men, who began to complain loudly. Then above the roar floated the voice of an ancient old man. "The magic millstones can help us," the old one cried.

"Yes! The magic millstones!" other men called out.

"What are the magic millstones?" a timid young voice asked.

"Show yourself," King Ari said to the person who had asked the question.

A boy stepped from the shadows. "I am Lars," the boy said in a strong voice.

"I will tell you the story," King Ari said, settling on a stone near the fire.

Long ago, when the crops had died and the people were starving, the god of the ocean visited a poor farmer. The farmer owned millstones for grinding grain. The people of the village would bring their oats and barley to him. He would place the grain between the two flat, heavy stones. He would turn the handle, and the stones would grind the grain into flour for bread. But the winter had been so long, there was no grain to grind.

"Your millstones stand idle," the god of the ocean said to the farmer. "You must use them to save the people of your village."

"How?" the farmer asked.

"Use them to grind your wishes," the god explained.

The farmer began to turn the millstones. He wished for bountiful crops and healthy calves. He began to grind. To his surprise, the millstones granted his wishes! Soon wealth returned to his village. The farmer saved his people.

"And that is the tale of the magic millstones," King Ari said to Lars. Then he looked at the ancient one.

"We must use the millstones to bring wealth again," the ancient one said.

"I wish we could." King Ari bowed his head in sorrow. "We have never been able to get the millstones to grind. If we cannot get them to grind, we cannot make a wish!"

Four sturdy men stepped forward. "We must try!" they insisted.

King Ari led them to his castle, which stood high on a cliff overlooking the ocean. He felt his hopes rise as they climbed the steps to a room in a tower. There in a corner lay the magic millstones, dusty and still.

King Ari and the men grabbed the wooden
handle of the millstones. "The stones will
turn, turn, turn!" King Ari chanted. "The
stones will turn and bring spring to our land!"

But the millstones did not turn. Desperate
to make them work, King Ari raced down from
the castle to the rocky shore. "O god of the
ocean," he cried as he waded into the freezing
water, "please help me turn the millstones
before my people starve!"

Maidens from the Ocean

t the instant King Ari's words left his lips, giant waves rose, whipped by the wind. Their white crests reached to the sky. In the midst of the waves, King Ari saw two women. He blinked in surprise. The women walked easily through the crashing waves. Their hair was a golden froth. Their eyes were as green as the sea. Shaking the seaweed from their shoulders, they strode through the surf breaking against their legs.

King Ari knew the women were not from the village. They wore long gowns that glimmered like the sea. "Who are you?" he asked in wonder.

"We are the daughters of the god of the ocean," they said to King Ari with voices as loud as the crashing waves. "We have come in answer to your plea."

"I am Marina," said the taller maiden.

"I am Elsa," added the fairer maiden. "We will help you turn the millstones. But then we must return to our ocean home."

"Thank you! Thank you!" King Ari said and quickly led them up the steep cliff to the castle. They climbed the winding stone stairs to the tower room, where the four men were still trying to turn the millstones. Their brows were covered with sweat. When they saw the two maidens, they stepped back in amazement.

"The god of the ocean has sent his daughters," King Ari told them.

"We will make the millstones turn," Elsa told the men.

"The stones will grant King Ari's wishes," said Marina.

"How can two women do what we men cannot?" the four men asked.

"Because we are the daughters of the ocean god," the maidens replied as they grasped the wooden handle. "We are as mighty as the waves and as strong as the tides."

The handle turned. The millstones turned. King Ari and the men were astonished. The maidens began to sing:

**"Grind, millstones, grind.
King Ari's wishes bring.
Grind, millstones, grind,
And hasten the spring."**

Faster and faster the stones turned. Soon King Ari heard excited shouts and cries outside. He ran to the window, leaned out, and felt a soft, warm breeze.

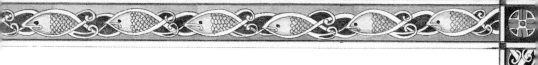

The sun was shining. The snow was melting. Icicles dripped from the tower roof, and green leaves sprouted on the trees. "The magic millstones are working!" King Ari cried.

The four men ran to the tower window to see why King Ari was so excited. Below them in the ocean, thousands of fish swam in silvery schools. On the shore the men of the village rushed to their fishing boats. On the beach young girls and boys darted after crabs and dug for mussels. In the hills above the coast, other villagers began to drive the sheep and cattle into the pastures.

King Ari rejoiced. The men cheered. Thanks to the maidens from the ocean and the magic of the millstones, spring had arrived! "We must celebrate!" King Ari called out. "We must give our thanks to Marina and Elsa, the daughters of the god of the ocean."

That night, a fire was built on the beach. A huge feast of fresh fish was prepared. The girls of the village danced in the warm ocean breezes. The men boasted about their fishing that day. The children gathered shells and played in the tide.

When all the people of the village had feasted, they sat on driftwood around the fire. In silent wonder they listened to King Ari's tale. He told them of his plea and how the god of the ocean had answered him. He described the daughters' beauty and strength.

"Elsa and Marina will make the millstones turn. They will grant our wishes. We will be wealthy and happy!"

A King's Greed

After the long winter, spring returned in full force. The sheep and cows grew fat on the plentiful grass. The people's gardens grew lush with barley, peas, and cabbage. The wooden boats grew heavy with fish from the warm ocean waters.

As he stood outside his castle and gazed upon his kingdom, King Ari frowned. For three days Elsa and Marina had turned the millstones. For three days the millstones had worked their magic. Now the maidens wanted to return to the ocean.

"Papa!" Nina ran up to her father. "Before Marina and Elsa leave, I want them to grant me a wish."

Laughing, King Ari caught his daughter in his arms. "And what would you wish for, my princess?"

"A pony to carry me into the hills!" she giggled.

"I think that is a good wish. Come. We will ask them before they go." King Ari led Nina into the castle. There his wife, Ingrid, met him.

"Husband, before the maidens leave, may I ask them to grant me one wish?" she asked.

"Of course," King Ari said, and the three hurried to the tower room.

"We must leave now," the maidens told the king when he arrived. "We must return to the ocean."

"Please, two more wishes before you go!" King Ari said. "One for my beautiful wife and one for my precious daughter."

The maidens agreed, although they were beginning to grow weak. They began to turn the stones, singing about a fine pony for Nina. Soon a whinny rang through the air. Nina ran to the window. "My pony!" she cried when she saw the frisky animal outside. Excited, she ran from the room.

"Wife, what is it you wish?" King Ari asked.

"We have food and good weather, but we are still a poor kingdom," Ingrid told the maidens. "Won't you please grind silver jewelry to make our lives sparkle with beauty?"

Slowly the maidens turned the millstones.

> "Grind, millstones, grind.
>   The King's wife's wishes bring.
>   Grind, millstones, grind.
>   Make silver bands and silver rings."

As the maidens turned the stones, King Ari's eyes widened. Silver necklaces, bracelets, and rings poured from between the stones and spilled onto the floor. With a cry of joy, his wife began to snatch them up as fast as they fell. "Now I will be so beautiful!" she exclaimed as she slid bracelets on her arms and rings on every finger.

King Ari sank to his knees. Grabbing handfuls of jewelry, he raised them high and cried, "We're rich!"

The maidens stopped grinding. Delighted with her treasures, the queen ran to show them off. The maidens bowed to the king. "We have granted your last wish. Now we go."

Jumping up, King Ari slammed the tower door shut. "No! You cannot leave," he ordered.

"But we granted your wishes," the maidens said. "The people of the kingdom are happy."

"*I* am not happy!" King Ari roared. "You must grind more. I want gold, elegant cloth, and spices! Then my kingdom will be the richest on the ocean! Grind me a roomful of riches. Then I will let you go back to the ocean."

With those words King Ari locked the maidens in the tower. The maidens pounded on the door. They ran to the tower window and stared longingly at the ocean. They saw the sea gulls flying over the ocean and felt the warm air on their cheeks. They heard the rush of the tides, and sadness filled them. Their strength was leaving. They needed the ocean.

"Tonight we must grind the king a roomful of riches," Marina said, "before we grow too weak to leave."

All night long, by the light of the moon, the maidens worked. By morning they had a roomful of shiny gold jewelry, spices, and silk for the king.

But when the king saw the glimmering gold, he was overcome with its beauty. "Now grind me a castle of riches!" he ordered. "Then a mountain of riches! Keep grinding and never stop!"

Chapter 4

Strong Warriors

Locked in the tower, Marina and Elsa grew weaker and weaker. Still the king demanded more riches. Slowly the maidens turned the millstones. No longer were they as mighty as the waves and as strong as the tides.

Working day and night, they made the king a castle of riches and then a mountain of riches. Soon the village was covered with jewels and gold. Then the riches spread across the pastures and into the hills. The riches poured into the ocean, scaring the fish away. The gardens were smothered under piles of gold. The villagers began to panic. Their sheep and cattle could not graze on silver. Even then, the king wanted more. Surrounded by his wealth, he forgot his people. He forgot his wife and daughter.

The villagers grew angry at the king's greed. The men of the village called a meeting. "We must ask the maidens to use their magic to stop King Ari," the ancient one said. "We cannot eat gold and silver. Our cattle cannot eat jewels and silk. The king must be stopped before we all starve!"

The men of the village marched to the foot of the stone tower. Calling loudly, they begged the maidens to grant the people's wish.

"King Ari's greed has turned him away from his people!" they told the maidens. "Please help us!"

"We will try," Elsa said.

The maidens summoned their strength.
Slowly they began to turn the millstones.

> **"Grind, millstones, grind.**
> **The people's wishes bring.**
> **Grind, millstones, grind,**
> **And stop their greedy king."**

As the maidens turned, strong warriors
leaped from between the stones. They carried
swords and shields and wore heavy helmets.
"Stop King Ari," the maidens told the warriors,
"and save the people!"

The warriors broke down the tower door and ran down the winding steps. Behind them Elsa and Marina stumbled from the tower. Holding onto each other, they made their way to the throne room.

"What is this?" King Ari cried when the warriors streamed into the throne room. He jumped up and reached for his sword. But his hands and arms were so laden with heavy bracelets and rings that he could not remove his sword from its sheath. The warriors drove him from the castle. Nina and Ingrid began to weep. King Ari fled to the mountains on horseback, leaving his wife, daughter, and riches behind.

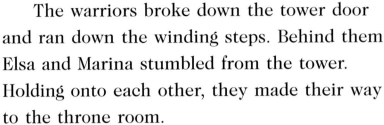

The villagers rejoiced. Once again the maidens had used the magic millstones to save them.

"We must go," the maidens said. As they walked shakily toward the beach, they gazed longingly at the rushing waves. But the warriors stopped them before they reached the ocean.

"No! You cannot go. We need you to grind us a ship!" the warriors said. "The farmers do not need us here. Our weapons will not plow gardens or feed cattle. We must cross the ocean to conquer new lands," they declared. "We need a ship and supplies."

The maidens had no choice. They were too weak to fight the warriors. "Bring us the millstones," Marina whispered.

A dozen strong warriors went to the castle and loaded the millstones into a heavy cart. Four oxen pulled the cart to the shore. The warriors unloaded the millstones and carried them to a dock that jutted into the ocean.

The maidens were weak, but the sight of the ocean gave them strength and hope. Once again, the maidens turned the handle and sang:

"Grind, millstones, grind.
Grant the warriors' wish.
Grind, millstones, grind,
And bring a mighty ship."

Slowly from between the stones came a longship with a billowing sail. The warriors watched in amazement. "You will go with us on the ship," the warriors told the maidens. "You and your magic millstones will help us conquer new lands!"

Grind On!

"No!" the maidens protested. "We belong in the ocean." The warriors did not listen. Grabbing rope, they bound the maidens and carried them onto the ship.

"Now the millstones!" the warriors cried. Straining and puffing, the warriors rolled the stones onto the ship and set them up in the middle of the deck. Finally the ship was ready to sail. The warriors began to row. As they rowed, they chanted, "Grind, maidens, grind. Make the millstones sing."

"We cannot grind with our hands bound," Elsa said.

"We cannot grind if we are too weak," Marina added.

The warriors untied them. The maidens rubbed their wrists where they had been bound.

Elsa and Marina were angered by the warriors. They realized that the warriors were as greedy as the king. The maidens knew they had to regain their power.

As the longship cut through the waves, Elsa and Marina stood on the bow. They felt the wind in their hair and the spray on their skin. The waves rushing against the ship sang to them, "The god of the ocean is with you! Grow strong, maidens, grow strong!"

Above their heads the seagulls screeched a message from their father—"Return to the ocean! Return to me!"

In the water below, a pod of whales leaped and dove. "Come back to us. Come back!" they called.

A huge wave crashed over the bow, drenching the maidens. As soon as the cool water hit their skin, they felt their power return.

The maidens went to the millstones in the middle of the deck. They grabbed the handle with their strong hands.

"Yes!" the warriors cheered when they saw them. "The maidens will grant our wishes!"

The maidens did not say a word. They knew that this time, the stones would grant their own wish. They began to turn the wooden handle.

"Grind, millstones, grind.
    Listen to our plea.
    Grind, millstones, grind.
    Send us back to the sea."

The warriors were horrified. "No!" they cried. "You must stay with us. We want more weapons. We want more shields. We want MORE!"

In answer, the maidens sang louder and turned the millstones faster.

> **"Grind, millstones, grind.**
> **Send the warriors salt.**
> **Grind, millstones, grind,**
> **And NEVER, EVER STOP!"**

From between the stones, salt flowed like a white river. "Stop!" the warriors ordered as the salt spread across the deck.

"You wanted more," the maidens told them. "You shall have more!"

Soon the entire deck of the ship was filled with salt from the bow to the stern. "Stop! Or we will stop you!" the warriors ordered. Angrily they pulled their swords from their sheaths.

The maidens only laughed. The salt was so deep that it reached the warriors' knees. When the warriors tried to come after the maidens, they tripped and fell in the white drifts. Still the maidens kept turning.

> "Grind, millstones, grind,
>   And hear our heartfelt wish.
>   Grind, millstones, grind,
>   And fill the warriors' ship."

Soon the salt reached the sail. It began to spill over the sides of the ship, carrying the warriors with it. Screaming, they fell into the ocean. Their heavy swords and helmets plunged to the bottom. The waves picked up the struggling warriors and carried them like driftwood back toward Iceland.

As the salt continued to flow, the ship groaned and creaked under the weight. It became so heavy that it began to sink. Still the maidens kept turning. With one last shudder, the ship tipped sideways. The heavy millstones tipped with it. They slid across the river of salt, fell into the ocean with a huge splash, and sank to the bottom.

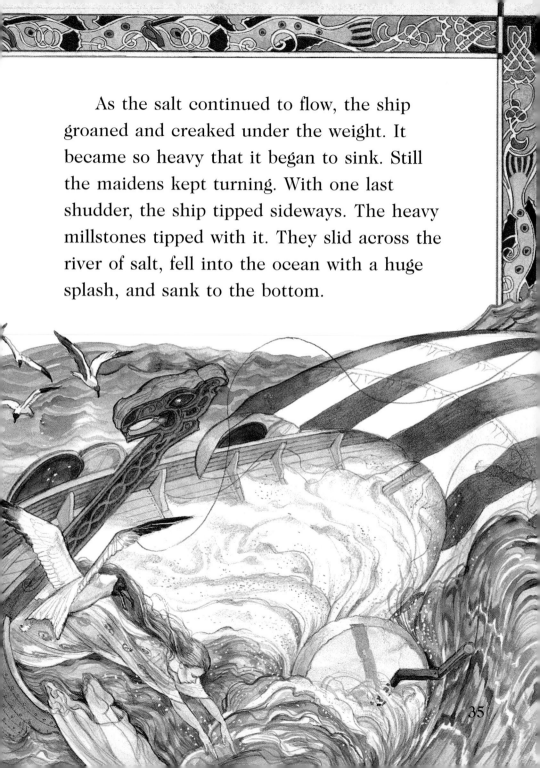

Now free, Elsa and Marina dove into the ocean. They watched the ship sink, its curved bow slowly disappearing in the waves. The roll of the waves rocked the maidens with love. The caress of the water filled them with happiness.

"You're home!" the seagulls cried as they swooped over their heads.

"We missed you," sang the whales as they spurted water into the air.

"Your father awaits you," the silvery cod sang as they zipped around the maidens, tickling their toes. The maidens swam deeper into the water. They dove with powerful strokes to the bottom of the ocean.

The god of the ocean hailed them from his rocky throne. "You are back, my daughters!" When the maidens saw their father, they wept with happiness. They were home at last!

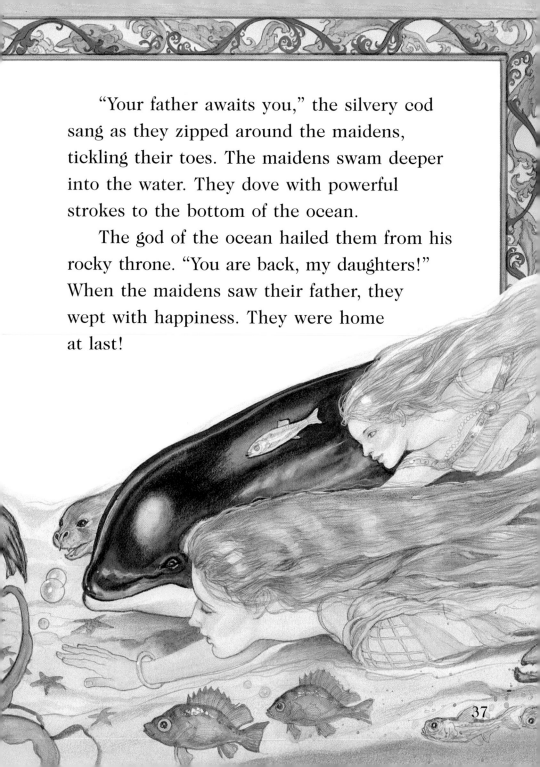

The maidens told their father the story of the king's greed. "When he captured us, we thought we would never return home," Elsa said, sadness in her voice.

"Then the warriors held us as prisoners," Marina said. "Fortunately, the magic of the millstones saved us."

"Your own cleverness helped as well," their father added with a laugh.

"What should we do about the millstones?" the maidens asked. "They are at the bottom of the ocean. They are still grinding salt because we told them to never, ever stop."

"Let the stones stay at the bottom of the ocean," he said. "That way, a greedy human can never use them. And let them grind on. Let the ocean grow salty. Whenever humans go into the sea, they will be reminded of King Ari's greed. Whenever they taste a drop of ocean water, they will remember the greed of the warriors."

The magic millstones still lie on the bottom of the North Atlantic Ocean. Even now, they are busily grinding. And that is why the ocean is salty.